PRAISE
be to You

Daily Reflections on Pope Francis' encyclical, *Laudato Si*
Published by the Sisters, Servants of the Immaculate Heart of Mary
Scranton, Pennsylvania

Praise be to You

Published by the Congregation of the Sisters, Servants of the Immaculate Heart of Mary, Scranton, Pennsylvania

IHM Center
2300 Adams Avenue
Scranton, PA 18509
Phone: 570-346-5404
Fax: 570-346-5439
E-mail: communications@sistersofihm.org

Cover design by Sister Fran Fasolka, IHM

Interior graphics by Sister Donna Korba, IHM

This publication may be purchased at amazon.com and barnesandnoble.com

TABLE OF CONTENTS

Laudato Si

Foreword
by Rabbi Daniel Swartz

What has been called "progress" has skewed out of control, leading, among other ills, to the inextricably linked challenges of climate justice and poverty. But there is at least one aspect of modernity that can serve as a source of wonder and hope: modern media makes it possible for the words of one person to be heard by everyone across the planet. Is it a sign of the Divine Presence in our lives that at precisely this critical moment, Pope Francis has chosen to address the world?

He writes (3): "Now, faced as we are with global environmental deterioration, I wish to address every person living on this planet…. In this Encyclical, I would like to enter into dialogue with all people about our common home." It is already clear that the world is listening and that this holy dialogue is beginning. In the few months since *Laudato Si* was released, I already have attended dozens of interfaith gatherings inspired by the Pope's words. Proclamations in support of the views expressed in *Laudato Si* have been issued by hundreds of rabbis, imams, Buddhist leaders, evangelical ministers and many more.

Pope Francis shows us a vision of a new—and yet, of course, at the same time ancient—view of what progress truly is. With God's help, we can fashion a world connected not by cell phones and social media, but by solidarity, justice, love and faith. Connected not only to other people but also to all of creation; connected not only to the present but also to all future generations.

The reflections that follow—one for each chapter in the encyclical, with each reflection divided into seven parts to mirror the unfolding glory of creation—are designed to help each of us deepen those connections. They are not a simple checklist

that makes the equation: a bit more recycling or a bit less air conditioning will solve the problem. Rather, they call us to deep, internal change—changing our viewpoint, our mindset, and most of all our hearts. If we want to stop the melting of glaciers and the flooding of lands, we need to melt hearts with a flood of love.

Will it be easy? No—it's always easier in the short run to be selfish. But, as these reflections on *Laudato Si* show, our lives become so much richer in love and blessing when we strive to act on behalf of the common good, when we consider the consequences of our actions to the "least of these."

This reminds me of a tale told about Rabbi Rafael of Bershad (1751-1827). Once, when he was about to go on a trip, he called to a student and asked the student to share his carriage. The student, Rabbi Shmuel, said, "I am afraid I should crowd you." Rabbi Rafael turned to him and said, "if we but love each other more, we shall have plenty of room." That is what we are called to do—if we love each other and all of creation more, there will be plenty of room for all of us on this blessed planet, now and forever.

Rabbi Daniel Swartz is the president of Pennsylvania Interfaith Power & Light, one of dozens of Interfaith Power & Light affiliates across the U.S., each working with individuals and communities of faith to address climate change from our commitments to faith, justice, and love. He is also the spiritual leader of Temple Hesed of Scranton, the proud husband of Rabbi Marjorie Berman and the proud father of Alana Swartz.

Laudato Si

𝒞𝒽𝒶𝓅𝓉𝑒𝓇 𝒪𝓃𝑒

What Is Happening to Our Common Home
by Chris Koellhoffer, IHM

Introduction

When astronauts flew into orbit in the 20th century and saw, for the first time, our astonishingly small, delicate planet from the perspective of space, they returned home as people forever shaken and changed. Standing in a new place allowed them to see Earth and describe it as living, rising, touchingly alone, a gleaming membrane of bright blue sky. That "glimpse of Divinity" universally evoked in the astronauts expressions of tenderness, awe, and gratitude for this living, breathing, fragile home of ours.

In the 21st century, Pope Francis invites us in *Laudato Si* to do more than step back and revisit earlier images of our Earth. The groaning of all creation in this time and place calls for an urgent expansion of our worldview and gives rise to critical questions: How might we see with new eyes so that our lives reflect a deep knowing that we are not separate from but in communion with all living beings? How might we foster an evolving consciousness of a universe unfolding and marked by commonality and interdependence? If Earth could speak to us, what might she say, and how might we most fully listen to and honor her pain, which is also our collective longing?

May our reflection on *Laudato Si* commit us to cherish and reverence the fragile, terrible beauty that is our common home, a home that holds everything we love, everything we know, everything we may one day dream.

Day One

*"Changes in climate, to which animals and plants
cannot adapt, lead them to migrate;
this in turn affects the livelihood of the poor,
who are then forced to leave their homes,
with great uncertainty for their future and that of their children.
There has been a tragic rise in the number of migrants
seeking to flee from the growing poverty
caused by environmental degradation." (25)*

When Serbian forces attacked Sarajevo in April 1992, there were one hundred animals in the Sarajevo Zoo. In November of that same year, a bear, the last surviving animal in the zoo, died. Little by little, the animals perished in spite of the heroic efforts of their caretakers, who had to run across open ground in plain view of snipers. One zookeeper was killed as snipers fired on anyone attempting to feed the animals. After 200 days of the siege, the lone surviving bear succumbed as much to the effects of war and regional conflict as to actual starvation.

More recently, the summer of 2015 brought fresh images of the effects of environmental degradation: desperate people on the move, hoping for freedom, food, safety, stability. This great tide of refugees risked their lives and the lives of their families on the dream, the hope, of a better future. War, bombings, regional conflicts, economic collapse, and extreme poverty destroyed people's neighborhoods, and those realities propelled them to leave behind home and the familiar. Many did not survive the harsh conditions of the journey.

Suggested Action
Send your prayer and healing energy to plants, animals, and people in our world who are uprooted, displaced, without a hospitable home.

Day Two

> *"Each year sees the disappearance of thousands of*
> *plant and animal species which we will never know,*
> *which our children will never see,*
> *because they have been lost forever…. Because of us,*
> *thousands of species will no longer give glory to God*
> *by their very existence, nor convey their message to us."* (33)

Growing up in suburban New Jersey, I eagerly learned the name of every flower, tree, and animal that inhabited our common ground. But my relationship with the created world shifted its perspective when a wise adult reminded me that, not only did I have the power to name these natural companions but that, "They have names for you as well." That statement changed my worldview from seeing myself as a caretaker apart from creation to knowing myself in communion with it as friend and neighbor.

It's the same perspective Marilou Awiakta voices in her poem, "When Earth becomes an 'It.'"

When the people call Earth "Mother,"
they take with love
and with love give back
so that all may live.
When the people call Earth "It,"
they use her, consume her strength.
Then the people die.
Already the sun is hot out of season.
Our Mother's breast is going dry.
She is taking all green into her heart
and will not turn back
until we call her by her name.

Suggested Action
Notice all living creatures you encounter today. As they observe your actions, what might they be naming you?

Day Three

> *"Some countries have made significant progress in establishing*
> *sanctuaries on land and in the oceans where any*
> *human intervention is prohibited which might modify*
> *their features or alter their original structures."* (37)

A sanctuary is a place of refuge, protection, rest. In the tradition of churches, synagogues and other houses of worship, sanctuary offers a welcoming place for people seeking asylum. We have seen this type of sanctuary recently in humanitarian crises of epic proportions, in the flood of suffering people pouring into Europe and in the throngs of families fleeing violence in Central America. The need for safety and security is universal and a basic human right.

Our sisters and brothers in the plant and animal world also need sanctuary. This type of sanctuary is created not in stone buildings or tented camps but in grasslands, coral reefs, forests. In ministering to the created world, we offer safe places where animals and birds may not be hunted or trapped, where native species of plants are carefully tended and protected, where the unique beauty, dignity, and value of all God's creation is named, recognized, and reverenced. In such a sanctuary, there are critical learnings which these neighbors and companions of the natural world stand ready to teach us.

In our common home, all of us share the desire to flourish that was voiced by Maya Angelou: "My mission in life is not merely to survive, but to thrive."

Suggested Action
Reflect on the created world around you. What is it that you cherish so deeply that you want to nurture and preserve it for yourself and for those who will come after you?

Day Four

> *"The good functioning of ecosystems also requires fungi,*
> *algae, worms, insects, reptiles and an*
> *innumerable variety of microorganisms." (34)*

Perhaps we're not overly fond of those beings that make their home in mold and dark, that wriggle or slither or sting. As an early morning walker, I've gradually befriended one of them: earthworms, those friends of the garden and nurturers of all things greening.

The trail I often walk is a place of natural beauty, bordered by lush foliage and offering an occasional welcome encounter with rabbits and deer. Not so welcome by me are the dozen or more earthworms struggling to propel themselves from the moisture and protection offered by grass on one side of the path to the dampness and shade on the other. In the middle of the path is unforgiving terrain, the gravel and asphalt of a trail made by humans. I have no idea what impels earthworms to attempt this journey, just that it can be deadly as they become covered in pebbles and dry dirt while navigating the dusty center path. Earthworms breathe through their skin and need humid conditions to prevent drying out, so if they don't cross the trail before the sun blazes, they will shrivel and die. Reluctantly, I've adopted the practice of picking them up and carrying them to the safety of the opposite side to which they were traveling. It makes for a much slower walk, but also a more purposeful and mindful one.

Suggested Action
Give thanks for whatever you might consider "the least of these" in the created world: those insects, worms, bacteria and fungi often invisible yet always supporting and enriching our common home.

Day Five

*"Let us mention, for example, those richly biodiverse lungs
of our planet which are the Amazon and the Congo basins,
or the great aquifers and glaciers." (38)*

In *The Sacred Balance*, geneticist and environmentalist David Suzuki observes that all aerobic forms of life share the same air. By our act of inhaling, we humans absorb atoms from the air that were at one time in the past part of other living creatures — rabbits, birds, fish, dinosaurs, cats and dogs, women, men, and children. This includes the holy ones who have gone before us: Jesus, Mary, Abraham, Mohammed, Buddha, Theresa Maxis, Pierre Teilhard de Chardin, Dorothy Day, Judy Cannato, and (here insert the great cloud of witnesses who have inspired your own life). With each inhale, we are breathing them in, up to 25,000 times a day. We can expand this scenario to include the likelihood that, long after we have passed from this Earth, those who follow us will be breathing us in as well.

Yet we are not the only ones breathing. The Amazon basin, the largest rainforest in the world; the Congo basin, the green heart of Africa; the bodies of dense glacial ice, the largest reservoir of freshwater on Earth: these lungs of our planet are also breathing in whatever we are breathing out. Will we exhale reverence, partnership, mindfulness, or the by-products of a thoughtless, consumptive pattern of living?

Suggested Action
Pay particular attention to your breathing. Breathe mindfully, aware of who you might be taking in with each inhale, and of what you desire to breathe out with every exhale. Be conscious that the manner in which you live and breathe affects our entire universe.

Day Six

"Today, however, we have to realize that a true ecological approach
<u>*always*</u> *becomes a social approach; it must integrate questions of justice*
in debates on the environment, so as to hear
<u>*both the cry of the earth and the cry of the poor*</u>*."*
(49) (Emphasis in original text)

When the poor of our world weep, our Earth weeps. When Earth is in pain, her people also suffer. It is not enough to grieve our individual acts of careless or thoughtless behavior towards our Earth. As we hear the groans of all creation, as we listen to the cries of our wounded planet, as we note the tears of our sisters and brothers who long for a more just, inclusive world, perhaps we are asking the insufficient question, "For what, for whom do we weep?" Perhaps the more significant and challenging question might be, "Who is served by our grief?"

In *Active Hope*, Joanna Macy notes that many times we describe either the problems we face or the solutions needed. She urges us to move beyond those two aspects and to focus on "how we strengthen and support our intention to act, so that we can best play our part, whatever that may be, in the healing of our world." This is the Great Turning, where we "pay attention to the inner frontier of change, to the personal and spiritual development that enhances our capacity and desire to act for our world."

Suggested Action
Follow the news reporting for one day. What are the cries of the earth and the cries of the poor that you listen to or read about in a day's news? What one simple act can you take in response to what you see and hear so that your grieving truly serves our world?

Day Seven

*"Our goal is not to amass information or to satisfy curiosity,
but rather to become painfully aware, to dare to turn
what is happening to the world into our own personal suffering
and thus to discover what each of us can do about it." (19)*

At the National September 11 Memorial and Museum in
New York City is a huge piece of artwork entitled, "Trying to
Remember the Color of the Sky on That September Morning."
Artist Spencer Finch hand painted nearly 3,000 pieces of paper,
one for each life lost, in re-creating the clear, cloudless sky, the
early autumn air, that was breathed in by so many as they went
about that morning. The grid of blue squares is accompanied
by a line from Virgil's Aeneid, "No day shall erase you from the
memory of time."

The suffering of people and our planet is multiplied daily, and
that collective ache becomes our own personal suffering. Still,
we move forward with hope, an audacious hope that insists that
present realities are not ultimate, that death and destruction will
not have the last word. We pray that all of us now inhabiting this
beautiful, fragile planet will live in such a way that no part of the
Divine creation will be forever lost, wasted, or forgotten. We pray
that future generations will also know the gift that is the glory
of a morning sunrise, the music of a songbird, the perfume of a
flower. With all that lives and moves and breathes in our Earth
community, let us work together with God's grace to fulfill the
promise, "No day shall erase you from the memory of time."

Suggested Action
Breathe. Remember. Act.

Sister Chris is a spiritual guide and author who engages in Mobile Spirituality Ministry worldwide. She offers retreats, presentations, process, and spirituality and enrichment programs connecting the soul of a group with the soul of the church and the world. Contact her at koellhofferc@sistersofihm.org

Laudato Si

Chapter Two

The Gospel of Creation
by Paula Gallagher, IHM

Introduction

Laudato Si connects us with a vast world of needs and blessings beyond our own doors. It makes us think larger than ourselves and challenges us to ask how we can sustain this earth together. After praying with Chapter One we are jolted with the shared experience of what is happening to our common home and the dire place we find ourselves. It is all the more distressing as we realize we have caused much of this predicament in our own generation by our speed and lack of foresight as we pressed for progress.

We are experiencing dis-ease with the magnitude of the mistakes we have made. There is a compassion fatigue being identified among all of us who try to serve the needs we see. We want to make compassionate response to these huge dilemmas. But the initial empathy that moved us so generously when we started tires in face of the constant needs we encounter. And that tiredness reaches a breaking point when exposed to the tragedies of the global village bombarding us with every newscast and headline.

Surely we must reach more deeply into our faith than ever before for wisdom and discernment about how to respond to caring for our common home. God is calling us. God has things to tell us. May this week's meditations call us closer to right solutions. Whenever we come seeking wisdom for life, God leads us on. We do not wander aimlessly amid all these challenges. Our Creator is walking this path of life with us, right here, right now. It is this God of ours who holds the answers to all our questions.

This week's prayer takes us into Chapter Two of *Laudato Si'*, "The Gospel of Creation." We search for Good News to balance our problems and give us wisdom about how to proceed. As we begin, we follow the steps of theological reflection to see, understand, act and celebrate this beautiful, wounded world of ours.

Day One

See

> " ...*human life is grounded in three fundamental, intertwined relationships with God, with our neighbor and with the earth itself.*" *(66)*

The power and hope of the Scripture comes in reminding us we have a God of new beginnings. Pope Francis returns us to the wisdom of the Biblical account of creation in Genesis. (65 – 66) We are at the beginning of time, with Spirit hovering over the chaos, about to launch creation. Genesis 1-2 tells of God's hand on each and every piece of our world, and his delight to find it good. We are the crown of that creation. Every human being shares the dignity of the Maker. We who hold the optimism of faith must never doubt Spirit can hover over the chaos again, still bringing forth the new creation.

Today's first step invites us to open our eyes and see. As you open your eyes today, behold again the goodness of God's creation. Let your love for this earth increase more and more. The seasons move reliably about us, each one bringing favorite sights, scents, sounds. But still there is a newness in each one that we have never met before. Especially as light comes and goes, there can be moments of such tender beauty that we are stopped in our own "*Laudato Si*" moment of praise. Watch for such moments this week.

This encyclical has a power to awaken our seeing on so many levels. We need every form of wisdom we can possibly gather at this point in history to meet the challenges before us. So today, we begin with the strongest wisdom of all—the Scripture. We are living the eighth day of creation. The Creator made something so good, diversified, and wondrous. It is entrusted now into the hands of our generation to carry forth in reverence and honor. May we do so with certain faith.

Suggested Action
We are conscious of the fragile, wounded world that cries for healing. But our antidote to this situation must be the optimism of our faith. Begin this week steeping yourself in the Scriptures, trusting this providence. See this situation as God does; there is nothing that is impossible for the Lord to restore, repair, revive, renew. So make your conversations optimistic and hope-filled. Help each other believe we will find healing ways forward to restore this beautiful world of ours.

Day Two

See

"Responsibility for God's earth means that human beings, endowed with intelligence, must respect the laws of nature and the delicate equilibria existing between the creatures of this world." (66)

Balance is everything. We learn that repeatedly in terms of our physical health and energy. When we do experience that balance, we move along easily, guided by Spirit's flow of grace. We try to be healthy, holy, mature human beings. We know the joy it is to be in tune with the Lord. Unfortunately we also know how challenging it is to keep that balance, to learn to live more steadily in the rhythms of God's grace.

Laudato Si challenges us to recognize new dimensions of how we have lost our balance. We are here to "till and keep the garden of this world. Tilling refers to cultivating, ploughing or working, while keeping means caring, protecting, overseeing and preserving." (66) As James Martin, SJ wryly notes: "We've done a bit too much tilling and not enough keeping." We have lost the balance of caring for our precious earth. We have drawn too wastefully upon its resources. We have taken steps in the name of progress which have reverberated in negative ways. We have upset the delicate balance of nature and have made choices that precipitate repercussions in the lives of others who share the planet.

Studying *Laudato Si*, we are challenged to do everything we can to restore that balance. Today continue our theological reflection asking to see the delicate balance going on all around us in the natural world. Begin by paying closer attention to earth's habit of changing seasons. Develop gratitude for the simplest signs time is beginning to turn—those particulars that tease the corner of your eye. Be aware we, too, are being called to change, to search for more careful, steady balance between our tending and caring.

Suggested Action
Make this reflection on balance concrete today. Ask the Lord to show you where your own body and being are in good rhythm and flow, or what adjustments you might need to make to become the healthy person you are intended to be. If you are able, put your feet on the good earth and get out to take a walk. Go asking God to help you see specific ways in which the delicate equilibrium of your own neighborhood is either being respected or ignored.

Day Three

Understand

> *"In God's loving plan, every creature has its own value and significance."* (76)

Understand more fully the mystery of this universe we share. Our faith perspective presents a God who is the Source of energy, setting everything in motion. The Creator's love, tenderness and affection can be felt in every single atom of creation. The Lord made an inexhaustible richness of variety and species. When we look closely enough, we understand the invitation the Creator enfolded in each unique piece to welcome its special gift with joy and hope.

In God's loving plan, each species of this magnificent world is interdependent in obvious or hidden ways. All parts are needed for fully functioning, thriving life. We need to understand the networking of life more thoroughly. None of us is self-sufficient. "We are dependent on one another to complete one another." (86)

In God's loving plan, media connections to the global village have their value and significance. The steady stream of calamities coming into our living rooms certainly stretches our compassion wide. But thank goodness media is also being used to take us where we personally might not go—inside the microscopic structure of a cell, to the bottom of the ocean teeming with amazing forms of marine life, soaring over the tops of mountains to see a vast, wide perspective. These things can help us understand the majesty of this creation and can make our own particular problems seem very small indeed.

Suggested Action
Seek ways to stretch your understanding of this wonderful universe. Begin with the familiar: in your mind's eye go back to a place on this good earth that is linked in a special way with your friendship with God. Was it a mountaintop with a sweeping vista or a meadow that felt like an embrace of God? Remembering these places is helpful, because they have revealed to us the beauty of God. Now seek a way to stretch your understanding into meeting and appreciating a landscape or a dimension of the creation that may be new to you. Try to learn something new about this amazing world of ours before nightfall. How does it, too, reveal the Creator?

Day Four

Understand

> *"God has joined us so closely to the world around us that we feel the desertification of the soil almost as a physical ailment." (89)*

Laudato Si certainly confronts us with the realities that challenge us. Here in the Southwest, through prolonged seasons of drought, we have concretely felt "the desertification of the soil as a physical ailment." We have had towns that have actually run out of water, having to truck a supply in to get them through the hottest part of summer. August 2015 we were heart-sickened to see the toxic orange sludge from the mismanaged EPA cleanup of an old gold mine spill out into our rivers. It poisoned the wells and acequias of the Navajo people's sacred land. And certainly those of us who call the magnificent Pacific Northwest home, or enjoyed being on mission there, were made almost physically ill watching those beautiful forests going up in flames.

The Holy Father makes direct essential connection between our heartbreak over the environment and our heartbreak over what is happening to other human beings. The two are integrally tied together. We need a concern, tenderness and compassion wide enough to hold both realities. We cannot remain indifferent to the cruel things happening to the land and its people. It is all woven together.

Once again, we must stretch our understanding. Pope Francis jolts us into deepening our knowledge of the issues we face today, so we can learn wise ways to respond. We can feel overwhelmed with the magnitude of the problems. It would be all too easy to fall over into compassion fatigue. It is all the more vital that we hold onto biblical hope. "Hope would have us recognize there is always a way out, we can always redirect our steps, we can always do something to solve our problems." (61)

Suggested Action
What specific environmental/ human situation are you
encountering that is distressing you almost as a physical ailment?

Pope Francis challenges us to "Cultivate the ecological virtues."
(88) Start asking yourself what this means. What is enough for
your portion, so you can share the rest with others who have
greater need? As you make it specific and particular, it will begin
the process of moving your understanding to action. What God
helps you to see, you must begin to do.

Day Five

Act

> "With moving tenderness, Jesus would remind them that each one
> is important in God's eyes." (96)

In the face of such large challenges, we must seek fresh and
innovative ways of caring for our common home. Sometimes we
wonder if our individual efforts can make much of a difference to
complex problems of this magnitude. But we must never forget
our Lord Jesus is the teacher of the mustard seed: "The Kingdom
of heaven is like a grain of mustard seed, the smallest of all seeds,
but once it has grown, it is the greatest of plants." Matthew 13:31-
32

Even now, young hands are taking hold of our future in the
Southwest. Our school children initiated a challenge to the city
council to eliminate all plastic shopping bags from our stores. It
took several months of preparation and training the public, but by
now we are all reaching for our reusable cloth bags. This gives us
great hope. These children are growing with a greater awareness
of the careful love earth needs.

Laudato Si presents us with many difficulties coming to crisis
point in our time. But people of faith steadily hold that with

great challenge comes great opportunity. Something vital is being precipitated now. A change of consciousness is coming. Whatever changes we can make, we must make them while we can, even if that be in the smallest, simplest ways. Let us put what we are learning in *Laudato Si* to good use. We are offered a shining hope for the future, but only if we learn to walk this earth with greater love and care.

Suggested Action
Focus the power of your prayer upon our children. We must pray in trust that this new generation will go on in a wiser way when we leave this earth. We must work to do all we can to hand them a worthy environmental perspective of care.

What can you do to witness this care to younger members of your family and ministry groups? Do they see you making simpler choices, being content with what you have and taking good care of things to make them last? Are they absorbing your patterns of treasuring, not wasting water? Are you showing them how to reach for products that biodegrade, and not lay toxins in the earth?

Day Six

Act

> "God can yet bring good out of the evil we have done. In infinite creativity, the Holy Spirit knows how to loosen the knots of even our most complex human affairs." (80)

This precious, beautiful, challenged world of ours is entrusted by God to our human care. This is not a time for desperation or compassion fatigue, but a time of conversion that prompts our hope-filled activity. We have to devise new, creative ways to develop and direct its resources. It is from this step forward we begin to restore a viable future for the earth.

We are acting collectively and decisively in some areas. Driving out in the Southwest, a common sight is solar panels atop homes, and mass solar complexes directed by our local power company. In the open plains of Colorado and New Mexico, wind turbines spring up quickly. Solar and wind energy are still new and expensive propositions, and we bear the burden collectively with rate hikes. Yet it is a positive sign that slowly and incrementally our energy needs are coming from healthy, clean, renewable sources.

We also need to focus acting particularly and locally. Every tender, honest act of kindness matters. Listen to the quiet power of our simple call to hold each other close. As we make the time to be with the sick and sick at heart, to feed bodies and spirits, we are remembering together that wellspring of grace that refuses to be extinguished.

We ache for time to find our way, to seek good, honest responses to the big challenges that face us. We have seen what happens to the arid country, both the land and our people struggling in oppressive poverty. There is such loss and grief it wears us thin with worry. But we must never feel we are not of use. Our Jewish heritage counteracts this with mitzvah, those everyday, essential, simple acts of loving-kindness that make the world go round.

Suggested Action
The real story of your life will be told by the footprints you have left on this earth and in people's hearts. How you step from this moment on matters very much.

Leaning into the reality we can do more together than any one of us alone, consider joining the Catholic Climate Covenant, (www. catholicclimatecovenant.org). There you will find concrete steps to form a care for creation team. This will boost your awareness of your carbon footprint. And step lightly into the spirits and needs of those right around you in simple, direct, appropriate ways. You have spent days of prayer seeing, understanding, appreciating how others are acting. Now go and do what it is yours to do today.

Day Seven

Celebrate

"The risen One is mysteriously holding us to himself and directing us toward fullness as our end." (100)

In *Laudato Si*, Pope Francis is a challenging teacher. He instructs in ways of understanding and acting that stretch our imagination. He reminds us of the grand sweep of diversity of this planet, its inherent radical interdependence. He squarely lays out the tragic predicament of this moment, so much of it caused by our foolish human push to power. In the ultimate perspective of faith, he shows us if we respond to the call to wake up and pay attention, these nightmares may yet be converted into miracles.

Thomas Berry calls this the great work we are called to, to continue the cosmos. This is one of those turning points in history. Our human progress is tied to the larger destiny of the planet we love. The great work of this moment is a transition from heedless destruction of the earth and its people, to a new manner of being caretakers of life. It is an immediate and urgent need.

So we explore these new forms of consciousness. We re-tune our minds and bodies into a continuous awareness of how all lives are linked together on this common planet. We must learn to approach each other in ways that venerate life.
Our call is to weave a protection around this beloved common home.

Life never stays static. We constantly move with new challenges. New possibilities lie ahead. There is only one way to learn how to live this new level of caring—to begin. Lord, walk with us. Keep us from giving up. Optimize our small efforts with your own internal energy.

Suggested Action
Remember as you wake up to celebrate every morning of your life. Be inspired to take on the great work of this point in history. Move with the challenges. Believe Spirit has us on the cusp of new breakthroughs in grace.

Be positive and energetic, even joyful, in your thoughts, conversations and actions about these issues. Ours is a God who loves mustard seeds. The little things we do mean a great deal. If we act both particularly and individually, as well as collectively and powerfully, we can care for our common home. Seize this opportunity. Be courageous. Step forward.

Sister Paula ministers in Adult Faith Formation and retreat ministry in the Archdiocese of Santa Fe, NM.

Laudato Si
Chapter Three
The Human Roots of the Ecological Crisis
by Kathryn Kurdziel, IHM

Introduction

I grew up in the country surrounded by immense beauty. Being poor I was taught from my earliest days to be respectful of the earth that fed us and the water that we drew from our well. Nothing was wasted. We saved and reused anything possible. We were proud of our simple three-room home, our large and productive garden, our shelves of canned goods put up each summer often after weeks of intense labor. Relatives from Philadelphia came to visit and marveled at the happiness of our simple, healthy lifestyle. So I was prepared to revel in the glory and privilege of caring for "our common home" as I reflected on *Laudato Si*.

However, unexpected challenges do arise, for the luck of the draw handed me Chapter Three—"The Human Roots of the Ecological Crisis!" I was plunged into the heart of darkness to ponder the sins of humanity: the disrespect for ecological integrity, the tyranny of technological overreach, the loneliness of excessive anthropomorphism and the ethical, cultural and spiritual crises of modernity. I sifted through the moral dilemmas that challenge people of faith to immerse themselves in the passionate struggle for our beautiful but wounded world. I shed tears of anxiety for the generations to come and only then did I gather real hope that steeped in prayer and thoughtful, meaningful conversation, humanity might find a way to embrace our common home and care for it and each other with compassion and love.

Day One

Technology: Creativity and Power

> *"Humanity has entered a new era in which our technical prowess has brought us to a crossroads... It is right to rejoice in these advances... for science and technology are wonderful products of a God-given human creativity."* (102)

> *"It [techno-science] can also produce art and enable men and women immersed in the material world to 'leap' into the world of beauty."* (103) But *"it has given those with knowledge and ... resources impressive dominance over the whole of humanity and the entire world... yet nothing ensures that it will be used wisely."* (104)

The growing and unbridled use of technological power forces us to call out to our Creator God as we face the possibility of terror of annihilation. But we do have choices. It is not too late to attune our souls to the restorative Spirit who gifts us with the desire and discipline to "renew the face of the earth." When the horrifying demons of terrorism, egoism, power mongering and nuclear devastation come toward us out of the future, let us cling courageously to Christ, our saving God, who simultaneously pulls us into the same future, fortifying us with responsibility, integrity, sound ethics, deep spirituality, and clear-minded self-restraint.

Suggested Action:
Begin the life-giving practice of daily contemplation. Accept Corrie ten Boom's conviction that a world almost totally devastated by Nazism could be transformed. Immerse yourself in her wisdom: "Never be afraid to trust an unknown future to a known God." Embrace the saving social action that presents itself in prayer.

Day Two

The Globalization of the Technocratic Paradigm

"Technology tends to absorb everything into its ironclad logic and those who are surrounded with technology 'know full well that it moves...
neither for profit nor for the well-being of the human race... (108)
'power is its motive — a lordship over all.'"
Romano Guardini, Das Ende der Neuzeit, 63-64 [87]
as quoted in Chapter 3 (108)

We can glimpse this ironclad grip where "our megastructures and drab apartment blocks express the spirit of globalized technology, where a constant flood of products [stuff] coexists with a tedious monotony" (113) where, in order to dominate, to gain a competitive edge, industries perpetuate hazardous working conditions and environmental degradation. This tedious monotony and suffocating flood of stuff drive "many to seek new forms of escapism to endure the emptiness" (113) they experience. Technology, potentially a wonderful gift, has become a conditioning agent generating "pollution, environmental decay and depletion of natural resources." (111) "It is based on the lie that there is an infinite supply of the earth's goods and this leads to the planet being squeezed dry beyond every limit." (106) Pope Francis challenges us to "refuse to resign ourselves" (113) to the hypnotic power of global technocracy.

Suggested Action
"Like a mist seeping beneath a closed door," let all that is authentic in us, quietly "rise up in stubborn resistance." (112) Find new ways to push against the high-tech culture that leaves us empty, restless and numb. Hide the cell phone; shut down the video games. Pursue instead an in-depth conversation with another human person.

Day Three

The Crisis and Effects of Anthropocentrism

"When we fail to acknowledge as part of reality the worth of a poor person, a human embryo, a person with disabilities…it becomes difficult to hear the cry of nature itself; everything is connected." (117)

"There can be no ecology without an adequate anthropology." (118)

Everything is connected! Perhaps it is this century's genius to have finely tuned instruments to examine the natural world and discover that EVERYTHING is connected in one grand thread of life. Awe comes first as the intricacy of harmony and design in the Universe presents itself to us. Humility and tears come next when we realize how often we have severed these delicate connections through ignorance, arrogance, violence and cruelty.

Hopefully, we will begin to understand that our egocentric lifestyle breaks the bonds of human interaction and destroys the intimate connections that wed us to our world and to each other. Our insensitivity and ingratitude for the things and creatures around us epitomize the disrespect and damage we have done to ourselves and others. We have impoverished our lives and decimated what is most precious in human existence. How could we not have known we belonged to each other? How could we not have seen our connections? How could we so have failed to love? We have sinned; we have gravely sinned!

Suggested Action
Compose an act of contrition that expresses deep repentance and resolve to reach out in humble restitution.

Day Four

The Value of Work and the Need to Protect Employment

> *"We were created with a vocation to work…Work is a necessity, part of the meaning of life on this earth." (128)*

Hebrew Scriptures open with God at work designing, perfecting and toiling to create beauty and diversity in our universe and on our planet. On the last day, God rested and enjoyed creation delighting in the perfection of each formation. Who can deny the pleasure of God on that day? God is our perfect model of meticulous artistry.

From the dawn of human existence, the human species worked to stay alive, to grow in skill, to share in social interaction, to develop creativity, and to experience personal fulfillment. Few things in life are more disheartening than losing one's job or being unemployed, especially over long periods of time. However, in our contemporary world, human labor and personal creativity are more and more disvalued as technology replaces human productivity and unique creativity solely for financial gain. Pope Francis urges us to "promote an economy which favors productive diversity and business creatively." (129) He insists that the creation of jobs and support of small local businesses and creative enterprises is "an essential part of service to the common good." (129) Employment upholds human dignity.

Suggested Action
Intentionally patronize local artists, farmers and small businesses even if it costs a little more. Get to know local vendors and encourage their hard work, resourcefulness and entrepreneurship.

Day Five

Practical Relativism

"When human beings place themselves at the center, they give absolute priority to immediate convenience and all else becomes relative." (122)

Do we notice the alarming and violent speed at which our world lives? Do we pay attention to the expectation that we will be served immediately? We do not like to wait in line, or wait for a senior citizen to finish crossing the street. Antagonistic tailgaters cause thousands of accidents each year. A store employee, a father of three, was trampled to death by a mob of Christmas shoppers competing for a popular doll. Junior high ball players seriously injured a referee because they didn't like a certain call.

Attitudes of heart such as these attempt to justify self-centered and destructive behaviors. Our ads aggressively push pleasure-seeking or power products that feed our feelings of entitlement. Entitlement culture militates against gospel mandates: "Love God. Love your neighbor. Be gentle. Have mercy. Forgive." When such values become extinct in a culture, Pope Francis warns that any atrocity is "collateral damage: exploitation of children, human trafficking, abandonment of elders, theft of organs" (Paraphrased from 123). Use, abuse and throw away become the norm, destroying nature, creatures and even human beings. The message of Jesus needs to be embraced if our earth and its people are to be redeemed.

Suggested Action
Monitor your insensitive and selfish impulses; substitute instead gratitude, patience, appreciation, tenderness or forgiveness. Advocate for the victims of our practical relativism.

Day Six

New Biological Technologies

> "When technology disregards the great ethical principles, it ends up considering any practice whatsoever as licit... A technology severed from ethics will not easily be able to limit its own power." (136)

The whole world benefits from sound research, from "balanced and prudent ethical judgement," (135) reliable and complete information and broad, in-depth consultation with those "directly and indirectly affected" (135) by biotechnical experiments. Great blessings have come from the research of science and technology which has enriched our lives. Biotechnology is a wonderful tool when it works collaboratively to enhance the natural order, but great care must be taken to protect and preserve the common good of the planet and its peoples. Especially important are those safeguards that apply to human life.

Immense responsibility belongs to the human community to diligently foster a culture of truth and dialogue. The same is true for communities of faith responsible for cultivating contemplation and moral vigilance. All creation is connected and interconnected; ALL IS ONE! We have the free will to choose ethically and unselfishly to cherish life on this planet or to permit all to be distorted and devastated because of our indifference, ignorance, desire for power, or lack of persistent, courageous action on behalf of the common good for present and future generations.

Suggested Action
Study everything, read everything, be aware of everything, be attentive to everything, pray for everything, dialogue about everything, act on what you see and know because everything matters!

Day Seven

The Saving Power of Interdependence

> *"Ecological culture cannot be reduced to a series of urgent and partial responses...There needs to be a distinctive way of looking at things, a way of thinking... a lifestyle and a spirituality which together generate resistance to the assault of the technocratic paradigm...To seek only a technical remedy to each environmental problem which comes up is to separate what is in reality interconnected... (111)*

Let us gradually intuit the redeeming forces working in our world among simple, thoughtful people who live authentic, interconnected lives recognizing that all creation is interdependent. In a glow of undying hope, may we encourage self and others to participate intelligently in the redemption of the world. Deliberatively, contemplatively, may we ponder the harmony and symmetry of all creation and prayerfully grasp the essence of beauty in such integrity. Let us gravitate toward those humble enough to control their power and resist their desire for dominance. Together, let us gently preserve the beauty of the earth by finding and making beauty wherever we are. May we cherish our carefully interwoven lives. Let us bow in awe and worship. Let our inner knowing prompt us to affirm Dostoyevsky's profound insight, "Beauty will save the earth." May we intentionally seek ways to counteract environmental degradation by fostering communities that live in truth, reverence and sacred conversation.

Suggested action:
Change a single perception. Study the dangers of genetically modified plants. Select heirloom flower or vegetable seeds and plant them next spring. Reverently sow them in the earth and feast on their beauty next summer. Then you will know what you need to do next.

Sister Kathy Kurdziel is the Director of Candidates and Novices for the Congregation of the Sisters, Servants of the Immaculate Heart of Mary in Scranton, Pennsylvania.

Laudato Si

Chapter Four
Integral Ecology
by Amy Fotta

Introduction

As I read and reflected on Chapter Four, memories of my life and work in Haiti—a country overburdened by environmental and economic struggles—quickly came to the forefront of my thoughts. Images of chaotic city life alternated with those of the country's majestic countryside. The seeming contradictions of life stayed with me in thought and prayer. Beauty vs. devastation. Joy vs. misery. Chaos vs. calm. None of these descriptions fully captures life in Haiti.

In fact, we all know that the realities of life, in Haiti or in our own homes, are far more complex than "this vs. that." In fact, this chapter reminded me of how closely connected I still am to the people and places of Haiti despite my physical distance from them. My decisions to care for and nurture my family, my community, and my environment are all connected to the larger world. In my fast-paced life of parenting, working, and teaching, I had lost sight of that. This chapter offered me a powerful reminder of how my life is intertwined with the lives of those who came before, those who are near and far, and even those who will come after me. I pray for continued mindfulness of this connection amidst the chaos of everyday life.

Day One

> *"Nature cannot be regarded as something separate from ourselves or as a mere setting in which we live."* (139)

It is easy to admire the beauty and majesty of nature. Admiring nature, however, is far different from regarding it as something inseparable from ourselves.

While I've always admired nature, I didn't see my relationship with nature as truly inseparable until I met an energetic youth group in a mountainous southeastern town in Haiti. They lived in a community that was suffering from the effects of severe deforestation. It was a vicious cycle: families needed more income than their farming provided, so they cut trees from their land to make and sell charcoal briquettes. The more they cut, the worse the soil became. Not only was the soil depleted and washing away, clean water sources were diminishing. Families walked miles each day to access water, and farming was increasingly more difficult. Worst of all, once trees were gone, they weren't replaced, which meant that income from charcoal was quickly running out.

Even though the farmers had not intended to harm the environment, their actions created a damaging imbalance with nature. Having experienced first-hand these devastating consequences of deforestation, the youth group, under the direction of an agronomist, set out to reforest their community and educate farmers on the importance of reforestation. The youth group understood their relationship with nature as completely intertwined: they relied on the land to nourish them as much as nature relied on them to nourish it. This understanding translated into a commitment to restore their environment. By doing so, they transformed their small community's approach to caring for the land.

Suggested Action
Reflect on the ways in which you are inseparable from nature.

Day Two

> *"Parents can be prone to impulsive and wasteful consumption,*
> *which then affects their children ...." (162)*

I read these words as if they were meant specifically for me!
Despite my best efforts to teach my three daughters to be
thoughtful consumers and to know the difference between their
needs and wants, we fall into the traps of our modern world:
overconsumption, materialism, and instant gratification. I say yes
to their wants without thinking or without asking them to think.

Reflecting on this opened my eyes to the disconnection between
my personal value of "living simply" and my actions. By allowing
my girls to over-consume, I am not aligning my values with
my actions, nor am I instilling the value of simple living in my
children. I could blame this inconsistency on the pressures of the
modern, materialistic world. Perhaps that is part of it; however,
avoiding the pitfall of "impulsive and wasteful consumption" is
exactly what will help my daughters make good decisions about
their needs versus their wants. More importantly, it will help them
learn the importance of measuring their self-worth and the worth
of others on who they are, not what they have.

Suggested Action
Consider the difference between your wants and needs. How
can recognizing this difference help you avoid "impulsive and
wasteful consumption?"

Day Three

"The pace of consumption, waste and environmental change has so stretched the planet's capacity.... The effects of the present imbalance can only be reduced by our decisive actions, here and now. We need to reflect on our accountability before those who will have to endure the dire consequences." (161)

Our world is full of compassionate, caring people. No doubt we compassionately respond to friends, family, and neighbors in need. We take action—donate money, collect goods, volunteer time—to alleviate their need. Many do the same even when strangers in other parts of our world are affected by natural or environmental disasters—drought, flood, illness. We are compelled by compassion to help those who suffer.

Pope Francis, however, challenges us to consider if that is enough. Is it enough to respond with compassion without reflecting "on our accountability before those who will have to endure the dire consequences" (161) of our imbalanced environment? Faced with natural and environmental disasters in our backyard and across the globe, we are called not only to aid others in need, but also to turn our gaze inward and identify our contributions to the over-consumption, waste, or environmental change that overburdens the Earth, our common home. We must acknowledge our own contributions if we are to respond not only with compassion but also with justice.

Suggested Action
Pray for insight into how you can reduce your own contributions to an imbalanced environment.

Day Four

*"A wholesome social life can light up
a seemingly undesirable environment." (148)*

Having lived and worked in Haiti, I have known families
living in desperate and barely humane conditions. I also have
accompanied many travelers on their first encounter with life in
this "developing" country. Inevitably, after engaging with the
Haitian people in their homes and neighborhoods, these travelers
always marveled at the joy radiated by the Haitian people despite
the physical poverty in which they lived. Some version of this
question frequently came up: "How can they be so poor but be so
happy?"

I, too, have grappled with this seeming contradiction. Perhaps
the answer to this question lies, as Pope Francis suggests, within
all of us, not outside of us. "… the limitations of the environment
are compensated for in the interior of each person who feels held
within a network of solidarity and belonging." (148)

The Haitian people show us that rich, human relationships do
have the power to transform "a hell on earth into the setting of a
dignified life." (148) Stripped of material riches, the richness of
human relationships thrives among the Haitian people. When we
value deep connection with others more than we value material
things, we too can experience the profound joy that is possible
through human relationship.

Suggested Action
Take the time to connect with someone today. Enjoy conversation
and the joy of human relationship.

Day Five

> *"Men and women of our postmodern world run the risk*
> *of rampant individualism, and many problems of society*
> *are connected with today's self-centered culture of instant gratification.*
> *We see this in the crisis of family and social ties and the difficulties*
> *of recognizing the other." (162)*

Technology. Cell phones. Social Media. Texting. These are just a few examples of what comes to mind when I think of our postmodern culture. Advances in technology undoubtedly have created incredible access to information and allowed for interconnectedness across the globe.

While these tools and modes of communication help us connect with others over great distances, they often disconnect us from the people and events right in front of us. How many times have you noticed this situation: family or friends out to dinner, each using a cell phone instead of having a conversation with one another? I see this or similar situations quite often: Parents, children, friends, families consumed with technology rather than with one another.

It's not necessarily a device or technology but the ways we use it that are problematic. As a culture, we are obsessed with these devices, the instantaneous communication and constant connection they allow us to have. While it is exciting to see technology advancing, it is risky to become so dependent on it that we become "disconnected" from those around us.

Suggested Action
Turn off your phone and see what happens!

Day Six

*"Once we start to think about the kind of world we are leaving
for future generations, we look at things differently;
we realize that the world is a gift which we have freely received
and must share with others."*   (159)

Indeed, when I reflect on how I may impact those who come after me, perhaps years or even generations in the future, I am struck with an overwhelming sense of responsibility. I must be a good steward of the natural resources that have been gifted to me if I want to contribute to a healthy world for future generations. I realize that conserving and protecting nature to benefit today's world is necessary but shortsighted; I must also make choices that will help protect our natural world far into the future. It is humbling to know that even though I am but one small piece of a much larger puzzle, I have a great responsibility to care for and share the gifts of our world with others—today, tomorrow, and many years from now.

Suggested Action
Identify one thing you can do now to help ensure that you will share the gifts of our natural world with those who will follow you. Invite others to join you in doing it.

Day Seven

"What kind of world do we want to leave to those who come after us,
to children who are now growing up?"   (160)

With three children ranging in age from one month to eleven
years old, this question is quite personal for me. Over the years as
a mother, I've already seen tremendous environmental changes.
One that sticks out in my mind at the moment is the ongoing
water crisis in the western U.S. To put it in perspective, when my
first daughter was born eleven years ago, the water shortage was
not yet a widespread reality (even though it clearly was a crisis in
the making!) Now, rationed water is a reality for many families in
California. What is yet to come? How will it affect the children in
my family?

This is only one example of how our natural world is changing,
but it prompts me to seriously wonder what the world will
look like for children growing up now. Pope Francis invites us
to ponder this, and he wisely words the question in a way that
makes us stop and think about the roles we all play in being
stewards of our natural world. He doesn't just ask what we want
the world to look like, as if we could imagine it but others would
be responsible for it. Instead, he asks us: "What kind of world do
we want to leave for those who come after us…?" In doing so, he
reminds us that we are personally responsible for envisioning it
and for taking action to make it a reality.

Suggested Action
Visualize what kind of world you want to leave for those who
come after you.

Amy Fotta lives in Scranton, PA with her husband, Marty, and three daughters, Tela, Eliza, and Ella Rose. She notes that, "In addition to being 'mom', I teach writing and recently started my own home business that has allowed me to turn my passion for helping others into everyday work. I also am an IHM Associate and feel blessed to be connected in this way to the IHM Congregation."

Laudato Si
ℭhapter ℱive
Lines of Approach and Action
by Annmarie Sanders, IHM

Introduction

Frequently as I pondered the challenges provided in *Laudato Si*, I heard the words of Jan Novotka's song, "Earth, Our Home," playing in my head:

We live on a wondrous spinning jewel;
so fragile and precious is she.
Oh Earth, beautiful one! Oh Earth, awesome and good!
Gentle planet, giving all; Oh Earth, our home!

I find the image of Earth as a "wondrous spinning jewel" lovely, but also compelling. What is our responsibility to come to know, care for, and deeply love this beautiful, awesome being? And what might this fragile and precious one be trying to teach us about life, about the universe, and about the presence of the Divine?

While Pope Francis urgently calls us to action as we care for Earth, he also invites us to see what science is discovering for us to explore and hold with wonder. As Sharon Begley writes in her essay in *The Hand of God*, the discoveries of science, particularly astronomy and cosmology, offer what only religion offered in eras past: solace and support. Science offers, she says, "a sense of wonder, and of awe; a sense that the world is rational; a sense, even, of the sacred. And, to believers, hints of the nature and character of God."

May our reflection on *Laudato Si* help us claim our responsibility for our wondrous, spinning jewel and in doing so, help us better know the nature and character of God.

Day One

*"Interdependence obliges us to think of one world
with a common plan." (164)*

For centuries, mystics, poets, and artists have tried to speak of our oneness with one another and with God. Mystics, writes Episcopal bishop John Shelby Spong, are people "in whom all boundaries have been removed" (*Eternal Life: A New Vision*). Mystics help us to see, Spong notes, that "we are part of who God is and what God is, and that God is part of who we are and what we are." Not an easy concept to grasp!

Cynthia Bourgeault helps us understand why we struggle with this idea when she writes in *Mystical Hope*, "We keep trying to express a vision of unity within a metaphysics of separateness. What is needed is a 'quantum' leap forward into a new way of seeing… so that we no longer focus on the separate things, but stare directly into the energy field that contains them all."

Imagine if we were part of a movement of humanity who began to live with the vision of the mystics—freed from boundaries— recognizing, accepting, and celebrating our oneness. We could do no other than to think of one world with a common plan.

Suggested Action
Thomas Merton had an experience while walking on a street in downtown Louisville where he suddenly realized that he was bound by love to all the strangers around him. "It was like waking from a dream of separateness," he later wrote of that moment. Reflect on an experience where you felt a profound connection with all of life. What might this mean for our work to care for our planet?

Day Two

*"…the post-industrial period may well be remembered as one
of the most irresponsible in history, nonetheless there is reason
to hope that humanity at the dawn of the twenty-first century
will be remembered for having generously shouldered
its grave responsibilities." (165)*

What would it take to become the age remembered by its
willingness to shoulder its grave responsibilities for the world?
How could we make it a practice to center every plan we create
and every decision we make around our concern for all of life, for
the entire planet, for the universe?

Author Jan Phillips suggests that we continually pose the
question: What is best for the whole? In her book, *The Art of
Original Thinking,* she suggests that the intersection of our
personal experiences with a global reality is the spark that can
ignite and fan the creative fires we need to motivate us to work
for the whole. "It is the recognition of our oneness that causes
the quantum leap to a higher level of thinking," she writes. She
goes on to tell of her experience photographing tide pools at
the ocean's edge. "I hovered over a patch of moss-covered rock
and photographed a piece of the action. When the photos were
developed, I was stunned. Every single tiny bubble I caught in
my lens reflected back an image of myself. Everything I looked at
looked back at me and contained me. This is the marriage of local
and global. It is all one…. All we have to do is remember, and live
in that awareness."

Suggested Action
Spend time with an experience in your own life when you became
aware of your own intimate connection with the whole of life.

Day Three

*"International negotiations cannot make significant progress due to
positions taken by countries which place their national interests above
the global common good. Those who will have to suffer the consequences
of what we are trying to hide will not forget this failure of conscience and
responsibility." (169) "… the poor end up paying the price." (170)*

In an airport as I awaited a flight to Bogota, Colombia for a
meeting of the Confederation of Latin American Religious, I
overheard a man from the United States speaking on the phone
of a recent luxury cruise he had just taken on the Amazon River
in Brazil. "It was fabulous," he exclaimed. "We saw such beauty."
In response to a question his conversation partner must have
posed, he added, "No, we didn't have to interact with the natives
at all. You don't have to ever get off the boat and they even have
blackened windows that protect your privacy. You see out, but no
one sees in."

One day later I was at a meeting with men and women religious
from throughout Latin America and heard other stories about life
on the Amazon River—from a much different perspective. One
was told by a missionary living on the banks of the river with
an indigenous community that lacked the most basic resources.
He spoke passionately of the growing and urgent need for
clean water, food, healthcare, and education, and he described
the devastating and rapid changes to the land caused by the
deforestation of rainforests. Looking into the eyes of us all, he
stated, "We are reaching the point of desperation."

Life on one river—viewed from two vantage points.

Suggested Action
Ponder the perspective by which you usually view hard realities.
Do you stay on the boat? Do you use blackened windows? Do you
place yourself in the midst of the harshness?

Day Four

> *Quick and easy solutions do not "allow for the radical change*
> *which present circumstances require." (171)*

Who doesn't know the temptation of an easy solution? A few moments on a grocery store checkout line next to the magazine rack expose us to a dozen quick solutions to vexing problems: get flat abs in 10 days, earn $50,000 without leaving home, discover the five steps that lead to happiness.

As alluring as easy answers may be, we know that life's complex problems require solutions that typically demand hard work, sacrifice, time, and often changes in attitude. The more we understand science and the structure of the universe, the more we can affirm Pope Francis' assertion that the problems facing the world today need solutions that allow for radical change.

An insight from Ilia Delio, OSF in *The Unbearable Wholeness of Being* sheds light on this: "Quantum theory reveals a basic oneness of the universe. It shows that we cannot decompose the world into independently existing smaller units. As we penetrate into matter, nature... appears as a complicated web of relations between the various parts of the whole."

If we are to help bring about within this complicated web of relationships the radical change required for the world to survive, we cannot be lured by the quick and the easy.

Suggested Action
Listen carefully today to any solutions you hear—whether they be from international policy-makers, local government officials, or your own co-workers and friends. Speculate on their effectiveness. Practice evaluating proposed solutions by considering their place in the complicated web of relations.

Day Five

"...there is an urgent need of a true world political authority ...
Diplomacy also takes on new importance in the work of developing
international strategies which can anticipate serious problems
affecting us all." (175)

The late Mary Daniel Turner, SNDdeN and I were walking
one Saturday morning in Rock Creek Park talking about the
mission of my place of ministry, the Leadership Conference of
Women Religious. "I'd love to see LCWR model the practice
of anticipatory leadership," Mary Daniel stated. "Anticipatory
leadership? What's that?" I asked. "It's a proactive way of leading.
Leaders, because of the knowledge to which they have been
exposed, are in a position to see more and have an obligation
to convey that larger view," she explained. "And they need to
convey not only what is, but what is possible." The exercise of
anticipatory leadership, Mary Daniel maintained, was one of the
most indispensable roles of leaders today.

Leaders, whether they be of religious congregations, corporations,
or nations can easily focus on the multitude of perplexing
problems that are immediately in front of them. However, as Pope
Francis notes, an urgent work of these times is anticipating the
realities ahead and working now to prepare for them. Many times
I have reflected on Mary Daniel's insight shared in that setting
of great natural beauty and have come to see that anticipatory
leadership—while time-consuming and difficult—is absolutely
essential if we are to imagine and then work to build a new and
very different future for the planet.

Suggested Action
Think of an upcoming meeting or a conversation you will soon
have about a matter of some importance. Is there a way of
spending time in that meeting or conversation on not just the
matters at hand, but on the learnings from the situation and their
implications for the future? What might you pledge to do as you
prepare for that encounter?

Day Six

> *"…political and institutional frameworks do not exist simply to avoid bad practice, but also to promote best practice, to stimulate creativity in seeking new solutions and to encourage individual and group initiatives. (177)*

The work of stimulating creativity and encouraging imagination is possibly one of the most critical of our time—and not always easy. Many forces in the world are structured to maintain the status quo, to lure us into thinking that the way the world works is just how it is, and changing it significantly is nearly impossible. For this reason, those who think differently and whose vision expands beyond what most of us see can be considered threats. Biblical scholar Walter Brueggemann commented on this in *The Prophetic Imagination* when he wrote, "It is the vocation of the prophet to keep alive the ministry of imagination, to keep on conjuring and proposing alternative futures to the single one the king wants to urge as the only thinkable one."

The work of imagination calls for stamina to maintain a vision in spite of pressures to do otherwise. In his book, *Creativity*, Matthew Fox wrote, "Creativity stands up to temptations to guilt for disturbing the peace. Many in a culture do not want to hear about innovation and new directions that creativity unleashes. Creativity takes courage."

Suggested Action
In our 2014 Chapter direction statement, we, IHM sisters, committed ourselves to "foster imagination, creativity, and fresh thinking"—a bold proclamation. Reflect on how you have been fostering your own and others' creativity and how that might have an impact on bettering Earth, our home.

Day Seven

"Our technical solution which science claims to offer will be powerless to solve the serious problems of our world if humanity loses its compass, if we lose sight of the great motivations which make it possible for us to live in harmony, to make sacrifices and to treat others well. Believers… need to be encouraged to be ever open to God's grace and to draw constantly from their deepest convictions about love, justice and peace." (200)

How wise Pope Francis was to remind us that, in this arduous work to save the planet, we cannot lose our compass. Perhaps one way that we can remember our motivations and our deepest convictions is to make it a practice each day to contemplate the beauty of Earth and the beauty of one another.

The late poet and author John O'Donohue in his book, *Beauty*, says, "When we lose sight of beauty our struggle becomes tired and functional. When we expect and engage the Beautiful… the heart becomes rekindled and our lives brighten with unexpected courage…. When courage comes alive, imprisoning walls become frontiers of new possibility, difficulty becomes invitation, and the heart comes into a new rhythm of trust and sureness…. Courage is a spark that can become the flame of hope, lighting new and exciting pathways in what seemed to be dead, dark landscapes."

Suggested Action
Make it a practice to contemplate beauty and allow the Beautiful to be your compass, your reminder of your deepest convictions about how we need to go forward to assure the fate of all life on this wondrous, spinning jewel we call Earth.

Sister Annmarie Sanders, IHM, serves as the associate director for communications for the Leadership Conference of Women Religious. She is the liaison from LCWR to the board of the Communicators for Women Religious and recently completed her term as a member of the board of directors of the National Catholic Reporter.

Laudato Si

Chapter Six

Ecological Education and Spirituality
by Margaret Gannon, IHM

Introduction

> *"Our common origin, our mutual belonging…*
> *and a future to be shaped with everyone."* (202)

These words at the beginning of Chapter 6 seem to me to summarize all of Pope Francis' encyclical. Each phrase gives us much truth to reflect upon in prayer.

It is new to me to recognize that all of us—humans, animals, plants, even stones—are God's children lovingly brought into existence in the Big Bang. It is humbling to think of myself, less than a speck in the glorious, ever-expanding universe, yet a speck continually and passionately loved by God! Lots to contemplate! All of us creatures of God's Big Bang belong in this universe and have a right to share in its goodness. Pope Francis centers his concern on the effects of ecological degradation on us human beings, especially those who are poor and most vulnerable to destructive climate change. Lots to call us to action!

That all of us share in shaping the future is inevitable. That we assure that we participate with all our sisters and brothers globally in shaping a supportive and beautiful future is our responsibility.

Lots about which to examine our lifestyle!

Day One

Toward a New Lifestyle

> *"When people become self-centered and self-enclosed, their greed increases. The emptier a person's heart is, the more he or she needs things to buy, own and consume." (204)*

How do I know if I'm self-centered? We've encountered persons in literature who are so self-centered that they are the author's objects of ridicule. Unfortunately, we probably have known some such persons in our own lives. But how do I know about myself? It's like trying to look into my own eyes.

Pope Francis gives a clue: the increasing need to have and consume is a symptom of self-centeredness.

As Pope Francis indicates, we live in a consumerist society, bombarded by enticements to buy. We are made to feel that unless we buy, the entire economy will collapse. What a pathetic economy that depends on the purchase of luxuries, excesses, junk!

Rarely the media prompt us to consider the common good. Yet that common good is significantly affected by our decisions; as the Pope states, "Purchasing is always a moral—as well as an economic—act." (206) Here's an excellent way to be counter-cultural: to work on maintaining a simple life style, to minimize as much as possible our intrusions on the common good. Pope Francis' Fiat can be our logo.

As I develop my simple life style, I will probably still be self-centered—there are plenty of things I want beside the material ones—but at least I will be doing less damage to the ecological common good.

Suggested Action
Identify one item you were going to buy this week and examine if
you really need it.

Day Two

Educating for the Covenant between Humanity and the Environment

> *"... an education in responsible simplicity of life, in grateful
> contemplation of God's world, and in concern for the needs of the poor
> and the protection of the environment." (214)*

Many of us are or have been educators, so Pope Francis'
statements on education are particularly important for us. I think
we could outline his comments as 'from action to principles and
back."

The earlier actions were efforts seeking to raise public knowledge
of specific threats to the environment and to limit those specific
damages. The Pope points out that the principles he now proposes
include a critique of "myths" such as individualism, unlimited
progress, etc. These are the myths that undergird contemporary
society and economy and try to justify the harmful impacts of
many environmental decisions. More positively, he proposes
principles that promote the well-being of all in an "ecological
equilibrium." Those principles are the bases for habits respectful
of that equilibrium and even an education that will "facilitate
the leap toward the transcendent" (210), and those habits are
evidenced in actions inspired by the principles of "ecological
equilibrium."

Our IHM tradition of fostering the arts is affirmed in the Pope's
inclusion of aesthetic education in his recommendations on
ecological education. He comments, "If someone has not learned
to stop and admire something beautiful, we should not be
surprised if he or she treats everything as an object to be used and
abused without scruple." (215)

Suggested Action
We are probably all involved in the daily actions the Pope
enumerates in paragraph 211. His list invites us to prayerful
reflection and action to contribute to the health of our planet and
our global companions.

Day Three

Ecological Conversion

> *"Living our vocation to be protectors of God's handiwork is essential
> to a life of virtue; it is not an optional or secondary aspect
> of our Christian experience." (219)*

When did your ecological conversion begin? Did it start with a
dawning awareness of the limitations of our planet's resources—
of the non-renewability of the fuels we use, of the reductions of
arable farmland, or the dwindling supply of water? For me, that
was in the '70s. How about you?

When was your conversion expanded by a recognition of the
global nature of the ecological challenges—the effects of climate
change on the survival of animals and plants, the proliferation of
greenhouse gases, the poisoning of the seas? Was that in the '80s
and '90s or maybe this century?

When did you come to understand that some of our human global
neighbors are suffering right now as a result of the harm we
humans beings have imposed on the environment? Maybe any
time since the '80s?

If you are young enough, you may have been born into
these understandings and didn't come to them gradually.
Congratulations.

What is the stage of ecological conversion to which Pope Francis is
now leading us?

"...[a] loving awareness that we are not disconnected from the rest of creatures, but joined in a splendid universal communion... the security that Christ has taken unto himself this material world and now, risen, is intimately present to each being, surrounding it with his affection and penetrating it with his light" (220-221).

May Pope Francis' words enkindle in us a sense of stewardship and protection for our planet and its people, "A spirit of generous care, full of tenderness." (221)

Suggested Action
Spend some time deepening your "awareness that each creature... has a message to convey to us." Try to focus on the message of one creature.

Day Four

Joy and Peace

> "To be serenely present to each reality, however small it may be, opens us to much greater horizons of understanding and personal fulfillment." (222)

All we need to know about joy and peace we can see in Pope Francis on his trip to the United States. Recall his willingness to meet the crowds, especially his manifest delight in children. He surely embodies "serene attentiveness, being fully present to someone without thinking of what comes next." (226)

The first pope to address the United Nations and the first pope for which a joint meeting of the US Congress was convened, Pope Francis demonstrates the gift of "being open to the many possibilities which life can offer."

Watching the Pope in the several liturgies makes it abundantly clear that he is a man full of peace. He affirms that "nature is filled with words of love." (225) Whether consoling the grieving family of 9/11, or expressing his solidarity with prisoners, Pope Francis shows us that "each moment is a gift from God to be lived to the full." (226)

I heard someone say, "It was as if Jesus were walking among us again." I think many of us shared her feeling. Wouldn't it be wonderful if that could be said of each of us as we go about our journey through every day! I think Pope Francis has given us some very clear hints about how to do it.

Suggested Action
Pope Francis proposes that we be careful about offering grace at our meals. He reminds us that "that moment of blessing… reminds us of our dependence on God; it strengthens our feeling of gratitude for the gifts of creation; it acknowledges those who by their labours provide us with these goods; and it reaffirms our solidarity with those in greatest need."

Day Five

Civic and Political Love

"Love for society and commitment to the common good are outstanding expressions of a charity which affects not only relationships between individuals but also 'macro-relationships' — social, economic and political ones." (231)

The theme of social and civic love prompts us to work collaboratively on behalf of the common good, both environmentally and socially. These two approaches are really one, as the Pope points out that the challenges of protecting and repairing the environment and the cries of the poor worldwide are not two problems but one. The environment must be cared for, both for its intrinsic value and for its role in helping people to shape and enjoy a healthy and fulfilling life; each person is indeed also of inestimable dignity and value.

Unity of understanding, purpose and effort equips us to address together the nearly overwhelming challenges. Pope Francis declares that "Social love moves us to devise larger strategies to halt environmental degradation and to encourage a 'culture of care' which permeates all of society." (231) He notes that such collaboration involves not only governmental activity, but all the projects and concerns of civil society: individuals and groups that put their talents and resources to the service of making their local, national or global communities more beautiful, healthier and safer. (232)

> "We invite others to join us in living out God's dream for this beautiful yet wounded world."
> - IHM 2014 Chapter direction statement

Suggested Action

Examine the environmental proposals and plans of the candidates for governmental office. If the candidates have little to say about protection for the environment, ask them.

Day Six

Sacramental Signs and the Trinity

> *"The universe unfolds in God, who fills it completely." (233)*

In these two themes, Pope Francis gets to the ultimate heart of the matter: God and creation. The truths are overwhelming and yet incredibly joyful and comforting.

The sacraments connect us with creation in very direct ways. They honor our humanity, indeed our very flesh—a unique demonstration of God's surpassing love for that humanity, embodied in each of us individually. The Pope describes Jesus's purpose in the Eucharist, "The Lord... chose to reach our intimate depths through a fragment of matter." He calls the Eucharist "the living centre of the universe, the overflowing core of love and of inexhaustible life." Therefore, he tells us, "The Eucharist is also a light and motivation for our concerns for the environment, directing us to be stewards of all creation." (236)

The love which the members of the Trinity share with one another overflows into the act of creating the universe. The universe is sustained by that same divine love. All creatures, from galaxies to hummingbirds, are outcomes of the eternal love of each member of the Trinity for the others.

Pope Francis proposes that relations among all God's creature should mirror the Trinity's love among its members—"a web of relationships." The world is following God's dream when all are in right relations with all. Clearly that calls for a loving and respectful concern for the well-being of our environment and for all with whom we share it.

Suggested Action
Welcome the God of creation in the Eucharist with attentiveness and joy.

Day 7

The Queen of Creation and Beyond the Sun

> *"At the end, we will find ourselves face to face with the infinite beauty*
> *of God… and able to read with admiration and happiness*
> *the mystery of the universe, which with us will share*
> *in unending plenitude." (243)*

In the final few paragraphs of the encyclical, Pope Francis remind us of models who can inspire and encourage us in our efforts to celebrate and support the integrity of creation. Mary, by her generous accepting of God's plan for her, welcomed Jesus into creaturehood. The Pope reminds us that "we can ask her to enable us to look at this world with eyes of wisdom." (241)

Joseph, the protector and provider for Jesus and Mary, knew how to collaborate with nature in the work of his hands. "He, too can teach us how to show care; he can inspire us to work with generosity and tenderness in protecting this world which God has entrusted to us." (242)

It is interesting that Pope Francis attributes the quality of "tenderness" to St. Joseph. That quality seems to be of great importance to the Pope. In fact, he states in *The Joy of the Gospel* that Jesus came to launch a "revolution of tenderness" in the world. We have seen the effect of that tenderness in Pope Francis' own person; he is a true participant in that revolution. We are called to join the revolution of tenderness toward all our companions in our global adventure.

Suggested Action
The last portion of *Laudato Si*, "Beyond the Sun," is so beautiful and encouraging that no commentary is necessary or possible. Just read it.

Margaret Gannon is a Sister of IHM who retired from Marywood University in 2014. She presently works with the orientation of newly arrived refugees under the auspices of Scranton Catholic Social Services and participates in the education of African sisters through the African Sisters Education Collaborative.

Daily Reflections on Pope Francis' encyclical *Laudato Si*
Published by the Sisters, Servants of the Immaculate Heart of Mary
Scranton, Pennsylvania

www.sistersofihm.org

Printed by Createspace